CW00584699

# ICC Uniform Rules for
# Demand
# Guarantees
## Including Model Forms
## 2010 REVISION

**Implementation Date**
**July 1, 2010**

**International Chamber of Commerce**
*The world business organization*

Second printing, with new cover.

Copyright © 2010
International Chamber of Commerce

All rights reserved. This collective work was initiated by ICC which holds all rights as defined by the French Code of Intellectual Property. No part of this work may be reproduced or copied in any form or by any means – graphic, electronic, or mechanical, including photocopying, scanning, recording, taping, or information retrieval systems – without written permission of ICC SERVICES, Publications Department.

**ICC Services**
**Publications**
38 Cours Albert 1er
75008 Paris
France

**ICC Publication No. 758**
ISBN: 978-92-842-0036-8

**www.iccbooks.com**

# Table of Contents

# FOREWORD

This revision of ICC's Uniform Rules for Demand Guarantees (URDG) is the first since the rules were developed by ICC in 1991. The original rules, URDG 458, gained broad international acceptance in recent years following their incorporation by the World Bank in its guarantee forms and their endorsement by UNCITRAL and leading industry associations, such as FIDIC.

This first revision of the rules was meticulously prepared over a period of two and a half years, and is the result of a collective effort by a number of ICC constituent groups. It was developed as a joint project by two ICC commissions – the Banking Commission and the Commission on Commercial Law and Practice – therefore taking into account the legitimate expectations of all relevant sectors. ICC national committees contributed substantially to the final product: some 52 national committees submitted several hundred pages of valuable suggestions on successive drafts, a large number of which were incorporated into the final text.

The ICC Task Force on Guarantees, which consisted of 40 members from 26 countries, reviewed the various drafts and added their own suggestions. The URDG Drafting Group, ably chaired by Dr Georges Affaki, met on a number of occasions, carefully reviewed all comments submitted by national committees and the Task Force and developed the final draft.

This collective effort has borne fruit; it has produced rules that reflect a broad consensus among bankers, users and all members of the guarantee community. In fact, the present revision of the URDG does not merely update the existing rules; it is the result of an ambitious project to create a new set of rules for the twenty-first century that is clearer, more precise and more comprehensive. As such, URDG 758 is destined to become the standard text for demand guarantees worldwide.

**Jean Rozwadowski**
Secretary General
International Chamber of Commerce
January 2010

# INTRODUCTION

The new URDG 758 succeed URDG 458. Over 17 years of practice (1992 – 2009), URDG 458 proved to be both successful and reliable. They were used by banks and businesses across continents and industry sectors. URDG 458 were endorsed by international organizations, multilateral financial institutions, bank regulators, lawmakers and professional federations. In contrast to the failed *Uniform Rules for Contract Guarantees* (URCG 325), URDG 458 reflected the reality of the international demand guarantee market and struck the most reasonable balance between the interests of all the parties involved. By choosing to instruct a guarantor to issue a demand guarantee subject to URDG, applicants renounced their ability to obstruct payment for reasons derived from their relationship with the beneficiary. In turn, beneficiaries were expected to state in general terms – but not to justify, establish or prove – the nature of the applicant's breach in the performance of the underlying relationship. Finally, because a demand guarantee is an independent undertaking, guarantors were assured that their commitment was subject to its own terms. They were insulated from the performance contingencies of the underlying relationship.

Their incremental use, backed by the support of ICC, enabled URDG 458 to make a critical contribution towards levelling the playing field among demand guarantee issuers and users regardless of the legal, economic or social system in which they operate.

Yet, URDG 458 formed the first attempt by ICC to codify independent guarantee practice. Over the years, the application of their provisions shed light on the need for drafting adjustments, clarifications, expansion of scope or clear corrections of the adopted standard. Views reported to the ICC Task Force on Guarantees from URDG users worldwide provided the necessary material to launch a revision of URDG 458 that both the lapse of time and the evolution of practice made necessary. The revision was launched in 2007 and was conducted under the aegis of both the ICC Banking Commission and the Commission on Commercial Law and Practice (CLP).

The ICC Task Force on Guarantees, the standing expert body created by ICC in 2003 to monitor international guarantee practice, acted as a consultative body to a Drafting Group that produced five comprehensive drafts during the two and a half year revision process. Each draft was submitted for review and comments to ICC national committees. Over 600 sets of comments were received from a total of 52 countries and were thoroughly examined. These comments were instrumental in shaping the new rules. Regular progress reports were presented to meetings of each of the ICC commissions considering the rules and were comprehensively debated. This method ensured that the revision takes into account views received from a broad cross-sector of concerned parties.

The resulting URDG 758 were adopted by the ICC Executive Board on 3 December 2009, following endorsement by the members of the two sponsoring commissions. They will come into force on July 1, 2010. The new rules apply to any demand guarantee or counter-guarantee where incorporated by reference in the text. They can also apply as trade usage or by implication from a consistent course of dealing between the parties to the demand guarantee or counter-guarantee where so provided by the applicable law.

The new URDG 758 do not merely update URDG 458; they are the result of an ambitious process that seeks to bring a new set of rules for demand guarantees into the 21st century, rules that are clearer, more precise and more comprehensive.

**Clearer URDG.** The new URDG 758 aim for clarity. They adopt the drafting style of ICC's universally accepted Uniform Rules for Documentary Credits (UCP 600) by bringing together the definitions of terms in one article. They also bring a much needed clarification of the process according to which a presentation will be checked for conformity.

**More precise URDG.** A number of the standards contained in URDG 458 left a margin for interpretation that varied according to the particular facts of the case. This was particularly true for the terms "reasonable time" and "reasonable care". The new URDG have excluded all imprecise standards with an aim to foster certainty and predictability. Examples are time durations for the examination of a demand, the extension of a guarantee in the case of force majeure, and the suspension of the guarantee in the case of an extend or pay demand.

**More comprehensive URDG.** Important practices were left out of URDG 458. This was particularly the case for the advice of a guarantee, amendments, standards for examination of presentations, partial, multiple and incomplete demands, linkage of documents, and transfer of guarantees. In addition, there was only fragmentary treatment of counter-guarantees. What was understandable at the time of the first attempt to codify demand guarantee practice can no longer be accepted 17 years later. The new URDG 758 now cover all of these practices and make clear that provisions governing guarantees apply equally to counter-guarantees.

**Balanced URDG.** The new URDG 758 endorse and build on the balanced approach that characterized URDG 458.

For example:

-   The beneficiary is entitled to payment upon presentation of a complying demand without the need for the guarantor to seek the applicant's approval. The new URDG also correct an unfair situation that would have left the beneficiary without recourse to the guarantee in the case of force majeure if its expiry coincided with the interruption of the guarantor's business.

-   The guarantor's independent role is expressed in stronger and clearer terms and, more importantly, it is now expressed in exclusively documentary terms. The new URDG expect the guarantor to act diligently. For instance, a guarantor is expected to reject a non-complying demand within five business days by sending a rejection notice that lists all of the discrepancies; otherwise, the guarantor will be precluded from claiming that the demand is non-complying and will be compelled to pay. Largely accepted in documentary credit practice under the UCP, the preclusion sanction is necessary to discipline unfair practices that work to the detriment of the beneficiary.

-   The applicant's right to be informed of the occurrence of the key stages in the lifecycle of the guarantee is acknowledged in the new rules. However, this information should not be a prerequisite for payment when a complying demand is presented.

**Innovative URDG.** The new URDG 758 feature a number of innovations dictated by the development of practice and the need to avoid disputes. An example is the new rule that proposes a substitution of currencies when payment in the currency specified in the guarantee becomes impossible. Another example is the new termination mechanism for guarantees that state neither an expiry date nor an expiry event. This solution is expected to reduce the number of open-ended guarantees that severely penalize applicants and are incompatible with the banks' capital requirements.

**The Guide.** The rationale, preparatory work and interpretation of each article of the new URDG 758 can be found in a separately released Guide to the rules (ICC Publication No. 702).

**The new URDG 758 package.** The new rules are accompanied by a model guarantee and counter-guarantee form featured at the end of this publication. They are destined to evolve into an indispensable companion to the new URDG 758 and their users. Experience shows that a comprehensive ready-to-use package that combines both the rules and model forms is more attractive to users than the previously separate ICC publications Nos. 458 and 503. It should also be conducive to more harmonized a practice.

In drafting the new URDG 758 model guarantee form, a unitary approach was preferred to one that would have consisted of multiple forms linked to the purpose of each guarantee. Tender, performance, advance payment, retention money, warranty and other types of demand guarantees share the same nature and have similar features. This was evidenced by the five nearly identical basic model guarantee forms in ICC publication No. 503 that accompanied URDG 458. Of course, URDG 758 users have the option of enriching the unitary model form with one or more of the clauses proposed at the end of this publication such as the reduction of amount clause for advance payment guarantees or even drafting any other clause outright.

**A final message: the need for clear drafting.** Clear drafting is the linchpin of a successful international demand guarantee practice. This has proven to be the case over time and across cultures and industry sectors. Using the new URDG 758 model guarantee form levels the playing field and avoids misunderstandings. As such, it will hopefully significantly curb the worrying tendency that some courts have shown in recent years to re-characterize demand guarantees as accessory suretyships – or the reverse. While sometimes warranted by the ambiguous terms used by the parties, such interference has considerably destabilized the international guarantee market by adding a particularly prejudicial element of uncertainty. Such a regrettable situation can be remedied by a consistent use of URDG 758 and their accompanying model form in any type of demand guarantee or counter-guarantee or, indeed, any other independent undertaking.

**Acknowledgments.** I would like to express my deep appreciation to the members of the ICC Task Force on Guarantees*, the ICC national committees and members of both the Banking Commission and CLP for their guidance, support and constructive participation in the revision. The Guarantees Department of RZB was very helpful in processing the hundreds of national comments received throughout the revision process and compiling them for the Drafting Group's review.

It was my privilege to chair the Drafting Group that undertook the revision. The members of the Drafting Group are listed below in alphabetical order:

**Roger Carouge** (Germany), **Sir Roy Goode** (United Kingdom), **Dr Andrea Hauptmann** (Austria), **Glenn Ransier** (United States), **Pradeep Taneja** (Bahrain), and **Farideh Tazhibi** (Islamic Republic of Iran).

Rarely has a chairman been blessed with a group whose members are so experienced and enthusiastic about the subject at hand, animated by team spirit, complementary in their regional and sectoral experience and able to endure with admirable patience the inevitable challenges of a fast-track revision process.

The result is the new URDG 758, which we proudly offer to the world.

**Dr Georges Affaki**
Vice-Chair, ICC Banking Commission
BNP Paribas
January 2010

* The Terms of reference and the membership of the ICC Task Force on Guarantees feature in page 41 of this publication.

## Article 1

## Application of URDG

a. The Uniform Rules for Demand Guarantees ("URDG") apply to any demand guarantee or counter-guarantee that expressly indicates it is subject to them. They are binding on all parties to the demand guarantee or counter-guarantee except so far as the demand guarantee or counter-guarantee modifies or excludes them.

b. Where, at the request of a counter-guarantor, a demand guarantee is issued subject to the URDG, the counter-guarantee shall also be subject to the URDG, unless the counter-guarantee excludes the URDG. However, a demand guarantee does not become subject to the URDG merely because the counter-guarantee is subject to the URDG.

c. Where, at the request or with the agreement of the instructing party, a demand guarantee or counter-guarantee is issued subject to the URDG, the instructing party is deemed to have accepted the rights and obligations expressly ascribed to it in these rules.

d. Where a demand guarantee or counter-guarantee issued on or after 1 July 2010 states that it is subject to the URDG without stating whether the 1992 version or the 2010 revision is to apply or indicating the publication number, the demand guarantee or counter-guarantee shall be subject to the URDG 2010 revision.

## Article 2

## Definitions

In these rules:

**Advising party** means the party that advises the guarantee at the request of the guarantor;

**Applicant** means the party indicated in the guarantee as having its obligation under the underlying relationship supported by the guarantee. The applicant may or may not be the instructing party;

**Application** means the request for the issue of the guarantee;

**Authenticated**, when applied to an electronic document, means that the party to whom that document is presented is able to verify the apparent identity of the sender and whether the data received have remained complete and unaltered;

**Beneficiary** means the party in whose favour a guarantee is issued;

**Business day** means a day on which the place of business where an act of a kind subject to these rules is to be performed is regularly open for the performance of such an act;

**Charges** mean any commissions, fees, costs or expenses due to any party acting under a guarantee governed by these rules;

**Complying demand** means a demand that meets the requirements of a complying presentation;

**Complying presentation** under a guarantee means a presentation that is in accordance with, first, the terms and conditions of that guarantee, second, these rules so far as consistent with those terms and conditions and, third, in the absence of a relevant provision in the guarantee or these rules, international standard demand guarantee practice;

**Counter-guarantee** means any signed undertaking, however named or described, that is given by the counter-guarantor to another party to procure the issue by that other party of a guarantee or another counter-guarantee, and that provides for payment upon the presentation of a complying demand under the counter-guarantee issued in favour of that party;

**Counter-guarantor** means the party issuing a counter-guarantee, whether in favour of a guarantor or another counter-guarantor, and includes a party acting for its own account;

**Demand** means a signed document by the beneficiary demanding payment under a guarantee;

**Demand guarantee** or **guarantee** means any signed undertaking, however named or described, providing for payment on presentation of a complying demand;

**Document** means a signed or unsigned record of information, in paper or electronic form, that is capable of being reproduced in tangible form by the person to whom it is presented. In these rules, a document includes a demand and a supporting statement;

**Expiry** means the expiry date or the expiry event or, if both are specified, the earlier of the two;

**Expiry date** means the date specified in the guarantee on or before which a presentation may be made;

**Expiry event** means an event which under the terms of the guarantee results in its expiry, whether immediately or within a specified time after the event occurs, for which purpose the event is deemed to occur only:

a. when a document specified in the guarantee as indicating the occurrence of the event is presented to the guarantor, or

b. if no such document is specified in the guarantee, when the occurrence of the event becomes determinable from the guarantor's own records.

**Guarantee**, see **demand guarantee**;

**Guarantor** means the party issuing a guarantee, and includes a party acting for its own account;

**Guarantor's own records** means records of the guarantor showing amounts credited to or debited from accounts held with the guarantor, provided the record of those credits or debits enables the guarantor to identify the guarantee to which they relate;

**Instructing party** means the party, other than the counter-guarantor, who gives instructions to issue a guarantee or counter-guarantee and is responsible for indemnifying the guarantor or, in the case of a counter-guarantee, the counter-guarantor. The instructing party may or may not be the applicant;

**Presentation** means the delivery of a document under a guarantee to the guarantor or the document so delivered. It includes a presentation other than for a demand, for example, a presentation for the purpose of triggering the expiry of the guarantee or a variation of its amount;

**Presenter** means a person who makes a presentation as or on behalf of the beneficiary or the applicant, as the case may be;

**Signed**, when applied to a document, a guarantee or a counter-guarantee, means that an original of the same is signed by or on behalf of its issuer, whether by an electronic signature that can be authenticated by the party to whom that document, guarantee or counter-guarantee is presented or by handwriting, facsimile signature, perforated signature, stamp, symbol or other mechanical method;

**Supporting statement** means the statement referred to in either article 15 (a) or article 15 (b);

**Underlying relationship** means the contract, tender conditions or other relationship between the applicant and the beneficiary on which the guarantee is based.

## Article 3
## Interpretation

In these rules:

a. Branches of a guarantor in different countries are considered to be separate entities.

b. Except where the context otherwise requires, a guarantee includes a counter-guarantee and any amendment to either, a guarantor includes a counter-guarantor, and a beneficiary includes the party in whose favour a counter-guarantee is issued.

c. Any requirement for presentation of one or more originals or copies of an electronic document is satisfied by the presentation of one electronic document.

d. When used with a date or dates to determine the start, end or duration of any period, the terms:

   i. "from", "to", "until", "till" and "between" include; and

   ii. "before" and "after" exclude,

   the date or dates mentioned.

e. The term "within", when used in connection with a period after a given date or event, excludes that date or the date of that event but includes the last date of that period.

f. Terms such as "first class", "well-known", "qualified", "independent", "official", "competent" or "local" when used to describe the issuer of a document allow any issuer except the beneficiary or the applicant to issue that document.

## Article 4
## Issue and effectiveness

a. A guarantee is issued when it leaves the control of the guarantor.

b. A guarantee is irrevocable on issue even if it does not state this.

c. The beneficiary may present a demand from the time of issue of the guarantee or such later time or event as the guarantee provides.

## Article 5

### Independence of guarantee and counter-guarantee

a. A guarantee is by its nature independent of the underlying relationship and the application, and the guarantor is in no way concerned with or bound by such relationship. A reference in the guarantee to the underlying relationship for the purpose of identifying it does not change the independent nature of the guarantee. The undertaking of a guarantor to pay under the guarantee is not subject to claims or defences arising from any relationship other than a relationship between the guarantor and the beneficiary.

b. A counter-guarantee is by its nature independent of the guarantee, the underlying relationship, the application and any other counter-guarantee to which it relates, and the counter-guarantor is in no way concerned with or bound by such relationship. A reference in the counter-guarantee to the underlying relationship for the purpose of identifying it does not change the independent nature of the counter-guarantee. The undertaking of a counter-guarantor to pay under the counter-guarantee is not subject to claims or defences arising from any relationship other than a relationship between the counter-guarantor and the guarantor or other counter-guarantor to whom the counter-guarantee is issued.

## Article 6

### Documents v. goods, services or performance

Guarantors deal with documents and not with goods, services or performance to which the documents may relate.

## Article 7

### Non-documentary conditions

A guarantee should not contain a condition other than a date or the lapse of a period without specifying a document to indicate compliance with that condition. If the guarantee does not specify any such document and the fulfilment of the condition cannot be determined from the guarantor's own records or from an index specified in the guarantee, then the guarantor will deem such condition as not stated and will disregard it except for the purpose of determining whether data that may appear in a document specified in and presented under the guarantee do not conflict with data in the guarantee.

## Article 8
### Content of instructions and guarantees

All instructions for the issue of guarantees and guarantees themselves should be clear and precise and should avoid excessive detail. It is recommended that all guarantees specify:

a. The applicant;

b. The beneficiary;

c. The guarantor;

d. A reference number or other information identifying the underlying relationship;

e. A reference number or other information identifying the issued guarantee or, in the case of a counter-guarantee, the issued counter-guarantee;

f. The amount or maximum amount payable and the currency in which it is payable;

g. The expiry of the guarantee;

h. Any terms for demanding payment;

i. Whether a demand or other document shall be presented in paper and/or electronic form;

j. The language of any document specified in the guarantee; and

k. The party liable for the payment of any charges.

## Article 9
### Application not taken up

Where, at the time of receipt of the application, the guarantor is not prepared or is unable to issue the guarantee, the guarantor should without delay so inform the party that gave the guarantor its instructions.

## Article 10

## Advising of guarantee or amendment

a.  A guarantee may be advised to a beneficiary through an advising party. By advising a guarantee, whether directly or by utilizing the services of another party ("second advising party"), the advising party signifies to the beneficiary and, if applicable, to the second advising party, that it has satisfied itself as to the apparent authenticity of the guarantee and that the advice accurately reflects the terms and conditions of the guarantee as received by the advising party.

b.  By advising a guarantee, the second advising party signifies to the beneficiary that it has satisfied itself as to the apparent authenticity of the advice it has received and that the advice accurately reflects the terms and conditions of the guarantee as received by the second advising party.

c.  An advising party or a second advising party advises a guarantee without any additional representation or any undertaking whatsoever to the beneficiary.

d.  If a party is requested to advise a guarantee or an amendment but is not prepared or is unable to do so, it should without delay so inform the party from whom it received that guarantee, amendment or advice.

e.  If a party is requested to advise a guarantee, and agrees to do so, but cannot satisfy itself as to the apparent authenticity of that guarantee or advice, it shall without delay so inform the party from whom the instructions appear to have been received. If the advising party or second advising party elects nonetheless to advise that guarantee, it shall inform the beneficiary or second advising party that it has not been able to satisfy itself as to the apparent authenticity of the guarantee or the advice.

f.  A guarantor using the services of an advising party or a second advising party, as well as an advising party using the services of a second advising party, to advise a guarantee should whenever possible use the same party to advise any amendment to that guarantee.

## Article 11

## Amendments

a. Where, at the time of receipt of instructions for the issue of an amendment to the guarantee, the guarantor for whatever reason is not prepared or is unable to issue that amendment, the guarantor shall without delay so inform the party that gave the guarantor its instructions.

b. An amendment made without the beneficiary's agreement is not binding on the beneficiary. Nevertheless the guarantor is irrevocably bound by an amendment from the time it issues the amendment, unless and until the beneficiary rejects that amendment.

c. Except where made in accordance with the terms of the guarantee, the beneficiary may reject an amendment of the guarantee at any time until it notifies its acceptance of the amendment or makes a presentation that complies only with the guarantee as amended.

d. An advising party shall without delay inform the party from which it has received the amendment of the beneficiary's notification of acceptance or rejection of that amendment.

e. Partial acceptance of an amendment is not allowed and will be deemed to be notification of rejection of the amendment.

f. A provision in an amendment to the effect that the amendment shall take effect unless rejected within a certain time shall be disregarded.

## Article 12
## Extent of guarantor's liability under guarantee

A guarantor is liable to the beneficiary only in accordance with, first, the terms and conditions of the guarantee and, second, these rules so far as consistent with those terms and conditions, up to the guarantee amount.

## Article 13
## Variation of amount of guarantee

A guarantee may provide for the reduction or the increase of its amount on specified dates or on the occurrence of a specified event which under the terms of the guarantee results in the variation of its amount, and for this purpose the event is deemed to have occurred only:

a. when a document specified in the guarantee as indicating the occurrence of the event is presented to the guarantor, or

b. if no such document is specified in the guarantee, when the occurrence of the event becomes determinable from the guarantor's own records or from an index specified in the guarantee.

## Article 14
## Presentation

a. A presentation shall be made to the guarantor:
   i. at the place of issue, or such other place as is specified in the guarantee, and
   ii. on or before expiry.

b. A presentation has to be complete unless it indicates that it is to be completed later. In that case, it shall be completed on or before expiry.

c. Where the guarantee indicates that a presentation is to be made in electronic form, the guarantee should specify the format, the system for data delivery and the electronic address for that presentation. If the guarantee does not so specify, a document may be presented in any electronic format that allows it to be authenticated or in paper form. An electronic document that cannot be authenticated is deemed not to have been presented.

d. Where the guarantee indicates that a presentation is to be made in paper form through a particular mode of delivery but does not expressly exclude the use of another mode, the use of another mode of delivery by the presenter shall be effective if the presentation is received at the place and by the time indicated in paragraph (a) of this article.

e. Where the guarantee does not indicate whether a presentation is to be made in electronic or paper form, any presentation shall be made in paper form.

f. Each presentation shall identify the guarantee under which it is made, such as by stating the guarantor's reference number for the guarantee. If it does not, the time for examination indicated in article 20 shall start on the date of identification. Nothing in this paragraph shall result in an extension of the guarantee or limit the requirement in article 15 (a) or (b) for any separately presented documents also to identify the demand to which they relate.

g. Except where the guarantee otherwise provides, documents issued by or on behalf of the applicant or the beneficiary, including any demand or supporting statement, shall be in the language of the guarantee. Documents issued by any other person may be in any language.

## Article 15

## Requirements for demand

a. A demand under the guarantee shall be supported by such other documents as the guarantee specifies, and in any event by a statement, by the beneficiary, indicating in what respect the applicant is in breach of its obligations under the underlying relationship. This statement may be in the demand or in a separate signed document accompanying or identifying the demand.

b. A demand under the counter-guarantee shall in any event be supported by a statement, by the party to whom the counter-guarantee was issued, indicating that such party has received a complying demand under the guarantee or counter-guarantee issued by that party. This statement may be in the demand or in a separate signed document accompanying or identifying the demand.

c. The requirement for a supporting statement in paragraph (a) or (b) of this article applies except to the extent that the guarantee or counter-guarantee expressly excludes this requirement. Exclusion terms such as "The supporting statement under article 15[(a)] [(b)] is excluded" satisfy the requirement of this paragraph.

d. Neither the demand nor the supporting statement may be dated before the date when the beneficiary is entitled to present a demand. Any other document may be dated before that date. Neither the demand, nor the supporting statement, nor any other document may be dated later than the date of its presentation.

## Article 16

## Information about demand

The guarantor shall without delay inform the instructing party or, where applicable, the counter-guarantor of any demand under the guarantee and of any request, as an alternative, to extend the expiry of the guarantee. The counter-guarantor shall without delay inform the instructing party of any demand under the counter-guarantee and of any request, as an alternative, to extend the expiry of the counter-guarantee.

## Article 17

## Partial demand and multiple demands; amount of demands

a. A demand may be made for less than the full amount available ("partial demand").

b. More than one demand ("multiple demands") may be made.

c. The expression "multiple demands prohibited" or a similar expression means that only one demand covering all or part of the amount available may be made.

d. Where the guarantee provides that only one demand may be made, and that demand is rejected, another demand can be made on or before expiry of the guarantee.

e. A demand is a non-complying demand if:

   i. it is for more than the amount available under the guarantee, or

   ii. any supporting statement or other documents required by the guarantee indicate amounts that in total are less than the amount demanded.

   Conversely, any supporting statement or other document indicating an amount that is more than the amount demanded does not make the demand a non-complying demand.

## Article 18

## Separateness of each demand

a. Making a demand that is not a complying demand or withdrawing a demand does not waive or otherwise prejudice the right to make another timely demand, whether or not the guarantee prohibits partial or multiple demands.

b.  Payment of a demand that is not a complying demand does not waive the requirement for other demands to be complying demands.

## Article 19

## Examination

a.  The guarantor shall determine, on the basis of a presentation alone, whether it appears on its face to be a complying presentation.

b.  Data in a document required by the guarantee shall be examined in context with that document, the guarantee and these rules. Data need not be identical to, but shall not conflict with, data in that document, any other required document or the guarantee.

c.  If the guarantee requires presentation of a document without stipulating whether it needs to be signed, by whom it is to be issued or signed, or its data content, then:

    i.   the guarantor will accept the document as presented if its content appears to fulfil the function of the document required by the guarantee and otherwise complies with article 19 (b), and

    ii.  if the document is signed, any signature will be accepted and no indication of name or position of the signatory is necessary.

d.  If a document that is not required by the guarantee or referred to in these rules is presented, it will be disregarded and may be returned to the presenter.

e.  The guarantor need not re-calculate a beneficiary's calculations under a formula stated or referenced in a guarantee.

f.  The guarantor shall consider a requirement for a document to be legalized, visaed, certified or similar as satisfied by any signature, mark, stamp or label on the document which appears to satisfy that requirement.

## Article 20
### Time for examination of demand; payment

a. If a presentation of a demand does not indicate that it is to be completed later, the guarantor shall, within five business days following the day of presentation, examine that demand and determine if it is a complying demand. This period is not shortened or otherwise affected by the expiry of the guarantee on or after the date of presentation. However, if the presentation indicates that it is to be completed later, it need not be examined until it is completed.

b. When the guarantor determines that a demand is complying, it shall pay.

c. Payment is to be made at the branch or office of the guarantor or counter-guarantor that issued the guarantee or counter-guarantee or such other place as may be indicated in that guarantee or counter-guarantee ("place for payment").

## Article 21
### Currency of payment

a. The guarantor shall pay a complying demand in the currency specified in the guarantee.

b. If, on any date on which a payment is to be made under the guarantee:

   i. the guarantor is unable to make payment in the currency specified in the guarantee due to an impediment beyond its control; or

   ii. it is illegal under the law of the place for payment to make payment in the specified currency.

The guarantor shall make payment in the currency of the place for payment even if the guarantee indicates that payment can only be made in the currency specified in the guarantee. The instructing party or, in the case of a counter-guarantee, the counter-guarantor, shall be bound by a payment made in such currency. The guarantor or counter-guarantor may elect to be reimbursed either in the currency in which payment was made or in the currency specified in the guarantee or, as the case may be, the counter-guarantee.

c.  Payment or reimbursement in the currency of the place for payment under paragraph (b) is to be made according to the applicable rate of exchange prevailing there when payment or reimbursement is due. However, if the guarantor has not paid at the time when payment is due, the beneficiary may require payment according to the applicable rate of exchange prevailing either when payment was due or at the time of actual payment.

## Article 22
## Transmission of copies of complying demand

The guarantor shall without delay transmit a copy of the complying demand and of any related documents to the instructing party or, where applicable, to the counter-guarantor for transmission to the instructing party. However, neither the counter-guarantor nor the instructing party, as the case may be, may withhold payment or reimbursement pending such transmission.

## Article 23
## Extend or pay

a.  Where a complying demand includes, as an alternative, a request to extend the expiry, the guarantor may suspend payment for a period not exceeding 30 calendar days following its receipt of the demand.

b.  Where, following such suspension, the guarantor makes a complying demand under the counter-guarantee that includes, as an alternative, a request to extend the expiry, the counter-guarantor may suspend payment for a period not exceeding four calendar days less than the period during which payment of the demand under the guarantee was suspended.

c.  The guarantor shall without delay inform the instructing party or, in the case of a counter-guarantee, the counter-guarantor of the period of suspension of payment under the guarantee. The counter-guarantor shall then inform the instructing party of such suspension and of any suspension of payment under the counter-guarantee. Complying with this article satisfies the information duty under article 16.

d. The demand for payment is deemed to be withdrawn if the period of extension requested in that demand or otherwise agreed by the party making that demand is granted within the time provided under paragraph (a) or (b) of this article. If no such period of extension is granted, the complying demand shall be paid without the need to present any further demand.

e. The guarantor or counter-guarantor may refuse to grant any extension even if instructed to do so and shall then pay.

f. The guarantor or counter-guarantor shall without delay inform the party from whom it has received its instructions of its decision to extend under paragraph (d) or to pay.

g. The guarantor and the counter-guarantor assume no liability for any payment suspended in accordance with this article.

## Article 24
## Non-complying demand, waiver and notice

a. When the guarantor determines that a demand under the guarantee is not a complying demand, it may reject that demand or, in its sole judgement, approach the instructing party, or in the case of a counter-guarantee, the counter-guarantor, for a waiver of the discrepancies.

b. When the counter-guarantor determines that a demand under the counter-guarantee is not a complying demand, it may reject that demand or, in its sole judgement, approach the instructing party for a waiver of the discrepancies.

c. Nothing in paragraphs (a) or (b) of this article shall extend the period mentioned in article 20 or dispense with the requirements of article 16. Obtaining the waiver of the counter-guarantor or of the instructing party does not oblige the guarantor or the counter-guarantor to waive any discrepancy.

d. When the guarantor rejects a demand, it shall give a single notice to that effect to the presenter of the demand. The notice shall state:

   i. that the guarantor is rejecting the demand, and

   ii. each discrepancy for which the guarantor rejects the demand.

e. The notice required by paragraph (d) of this article shall be sent without delay but not later than the close of the fifth business day following the day of presentation.

f.  A guarantor failing to act in accordance with paragraphs (d) or (e) of this article shall be precluded from claiming that the demand and any related documents do not constitute a complying demand.

g.  The guarantor may at any time, after providing the notice required in paragraph (d) of this article, return any documents presented in paper form to the presenter and dispose of the electronic records in any manner that it considers appropriate without incurring any responsibility.

h.  For the purpose of paragraphs (d), (f) and (g) of this article, guarantor includes counter-guarantor.

## Article 25
## Reduction and termination

a.  The amount payable under the guarantee shall be reduced by any amount:

i.   paid under the guarantee,

ii.  resulting from the application of article 13, or

iii. indicated in the beneficiary's signed partial release from liability under the guarantee.

b.  Whether or not the guarantee document is returned to the guarantor, the guarantee shall terminate:

i.   on expiry,

ii.  when no amount remains payable under it, or

iii. on presentation to the guarantor of the beneficiary's signed release from liability under the guarantee.

c.  If the guarantee or the counter-guarantee states neither an expiry date nor an expiry event, the guarantee shall terminate after the lapse of three years from the date of issue and the counter-guarantee shall terminate 30 calendar days after the guarantee terminates.

d.  If the expiry date of a guarantee falls on a day that is not a business day at the place for presentation of the demand, the expiry date is extended to the first following business day at that place.

e.  Where, to the knowledge of the guarantor, the guarantee terminates as a result of any of the reasons indicated in paragraph (b) above, but other than because of the advent of the expiry date, the guarantor shall without delay so inform the instructing party or, where applicable, the counter-guarantor and, in that case, the counter-guarantor shall so inform the instructing party.

## Article 26

## Force majeure

a. In this article, "force majeure" means acts of God, riots, civil commotions, insurrections, wars, acts of terrorism or any causes beyond the control of the guarantor or counter-guarantor that interrupt its business as it relates to acts of a kind subject to these rules.

b. Should the guarantee expire at a time when presentation or payment under that guarantee is prevented by force majeure:

   i. each of the guarantee and any counter-guarantee shall be extended for a period of 30 calendar days from the date on which it would otherwise have expired, and the guarantor shall as soon as practicable inform the instructing party or, in the case of a counter-guarantee, the counter-guarantor of the force majeure and the extension, and the counter-guarantor shall so inform the instructing party;

   ii. the running of the time for examination under article 20 of a presentation made but not yet examined before the force majeure shall be suspended until the resumption of the guarantor's business; and

   iii. a complying demand under the guarantee presented before the force majeure but not paid because of the force majeure shall be paid when the force majeure ceases even if that guarantee has expired, and in this situation the guarantor shall be entitled to present a demand under the counter-guarantee within 30 calendar days after cessation of the force majeure even if the counter-guarantee has expired.

c. Should the counter-guarantee expire at a time when presentation or payment under that counter-guarantee is prevented by force majeure:

   i.   the counter-guarantee shall be extended for a period of 30 calendar days from the date on which the counter-guarantor informs the guarantor of the cessation of the force majeure. The counter-guarantor shall then inform the instructing party of the force majeure and the extension;

  ii.  the running of the time for examination under article 20 of a presentation made but not yet examined before the force majeure shall be suspended until the resumption of the counter-guarantor's business; and

 iii. a complying demand under the counter-guarantee presented before the force majeure but not paid because of the force majeure shall be paid when the force majeure ceases even if that counter-guarantee has expired.

d.  The instructing party shall be bound by any extension, suspension or payment under this article.

e.  The guarantor and the counter-guarantor assume no further liability for the consequences of the force majeure.

## Article 27

## Disclaimer on effectiveness of documents

The guarantor assumes no liability or responsibility for:

a.  The form, sufficiency, accuracy, genuineness, falsification, or legal effect of any signature or document presented to it;

b.  The general or particular statements made in, or superimposed on, any document presented to it;

c.  The description, quantity, weight, quality, condition, packing, delivery, value or existence of the goods, services or other performance or data represented by or referred to in any document presented to it; or

d.  The good faith, acts, omissions, solvency, performance or standing of any person issuing or referred to in any other capacity in any document presented to it.

## Article 28
### Disclaimer on transmission and translation

a. The guarantor assumes no liability or responsibility for the consequences of delay, loss in transit, mutilation or other errors arising in the transmission of any document, if that document is transmitted or sent according to the requirements stated in the guarantee, or when the guarantor may have taken the initiative in the choice of the delivery service in the absence of instructions to that effect.

b. The guarantor assumes no liability or responsibility for errors in translation or interpretation of technical terms and may transmit all or part of the guarantee text without translating it.

## Article 29
### Disclaimer for acts of another party

A guarantor using the services of another party for the purpose of giving effect to the instructions of an instructing party or counter-guarantor does so for the account and at the risk of that instructing party or counter-guarantor.

## Article 30
### Limits on exemption from liability

Articles 27 to 29 shall not exempt a guarantor from liability or responsibility for its failure to act in good faith.

## Article 31
### Indemnity for foreign laws and usages

The instructing party or, in the case of a counter-guarantee, the counter-guarantor shall indemnify the guarantor against all obligations and responsibilities imposed by foreign laws and usages, including where those foreign laws and usages impose terms into the guarantee or the counter-guarantee that override its specified terms. The instructing party shall indemnify the counter-guarantor that has indemnified the guarantor under this article.

## Article 32

## Liability for charges

a. A party instructing another party to perform services under these rules is liable to pay that party's charges for carrying out its instructions.

b. If a guarantee states that charges are for the account of the beneficiary and those charges cannot be collected, the instructing party is liable to pay those charges. If a counter-guarantee states that charges relating to the guarantee are for the account of the beneficiary and those charges cannot be collected, the counter-guarantor remains liable to the guarantor, and the instructing party to the counter-guarantor, to pay those charges.

c. Neither the guarantor nor any advising party should stipulate that the guarantee, or any advice or amendment of it, is conditional upon the receipt by the guarantor or any advising party of its charges.

## Article 33

## Transfer of guarantee and assignment of proceeds

a. A guarantee is transferable only if it specifically states that it is "transferable", in which case it may be transferred more than once for the full amount available at the time of transfer. A counter-guarantee is not transferable.

b. Even if a guarantee specifically states that it is transferable, the guarantor is not obliged to give effect to a request to transfer that guarantee after its issue except to the extent and in the manner expressly consented to by the guarantor.

c. A transferable guarantee means a guarantee that may be made available by the guarantor to a new beneficiary ("transferee") at the request of the existing beneficiary ("transferor").

d. The following provisions apply to the transfer of a guarantee:

  i. a transferred guarantee shall include all amendments to which the transferor and guarantor have agreed as of the date of transfer; and

  ii. a guarantee can only be transferred where, in addition to the conditions stated in paragraphs (a), (b) and (d)(i) of this article, the transferor has provided a signed statement to the guarantor that the transferee has acquired the transferor's rights and obligations in the underlying relationship.

e.  Unless otherwise agreed at the time of transfer, the transferor shall pay all charges incurred for the transfer.

f.  Under a transferred guarantee, a demand and any supporting statement shall be signed by the transferee. Unless the guarantee provides otherwise, the name and the signature of the transferee may be used in place of the name and signature of the transferor in any other document.

g.  Whether or not the guarantee states that it is transferable, and subject to the provisions of the applicable law:

    i.   the beneficiary may assign any proceeds to which it may be or may become entitled under the guarantee;

    ii.  however, the guarantor shall not be obliged to pay an assignee of these proceeds unless the guarantor has agreed to do so.

## Article 34
## Governing law

a.  Unless otherwise provided in the guarantee, its governing law shall be that of the location of the guarantor's branch or office that issued the guarantee.

b.  Unless otherwise provided in the counter-guarantee, its governing law shall be that of the location of the counter-guarantor's branch or office that issued the counter-guarantee.

## Article 35
## Jurisdiction

a.  Unless otherwise provided in the guarantee, any dispute between the guarantor and the beneficiary relating to the guarantee shall be settled exclusively by the competent court of the country of the location of the guarantor's branch or office that issued the guarantee.

b.  Unless otherwise provided in the counter-guarantee, any dispute between the counter-guarantor and the guarantor relating to the counter-guarantee shall be settled exclusively by the competent court of the country of the location of the counter-guarantor's branch or office that issued the counter-guarantee.

# Appendices

## Form of Demand Guarantee under URDG 758[*]

[*Guarantor Letterhead or SWIFT identifier Code*]

To: [*Insert name and contact information of the Beneficiary*]

Date: [*Insert date of issue*]

- **Type of guarantee:** [*Specify tender guarantee, advance payment guarantee, performance guarantee, payment guarantee, retention money guarantee, warranty guarantee etc.*]
- **Guarantee No.** [*Insert guarantee reference number*]
- **The Guarantor:** [*Insert name and address of place of issue, unless indicated in the letterhead*]
- **The Applicant:** [*Insert name and address*]
- **The Beneficiary:** [*Insert name and address*]
- **The Underlying Relationship:** The Applicant's obligation in respect of [*Insert reference number or other information identifying the contract, tender conditions or other relationship between the applicant and the beneficiary on which the guarantee is based*]
- **Guarantee Amount and currency:** [*Insert in figures and words the maximum amount payable and the currency in which it is payable*]
- **Any document required in support of the demand for payment, apart from the supporting statement that is explicitly required in the text below:** [*Insert any additional document required in support of the demand for payment. If the guarantee requires no documents other than the demand and the supporting statement, keep this space empty or indicate "none"*]

---

[*] The Form of Demand Guarantee and Counter-Guarantee under URDG 758 as well as the Optional Clauses proposed in the following pages are provided for guidance. They are not part of the rules.

- **LANGUAGE OF ANY REQUIRED DOCUMENTS:** [*Insert the language of any required document. Documents to be issued by the applicant or the beneficiary shall be in the language of the guarantee unless otherwise indicated herein*]
- **FORM OF PRESENTATION:** [*Insert paper or electronic form. If paper, indicate mode of delivery. If electronic, indicate the format, the system for data delivery and the electronic address for presentation*]
- **PLACE FOR PRESENTATION:** [*Guarantor to insert address of branch where a paper presentation is to be made or, in the case of an electronic presentation, an electronic address such as the Guarantor's SWIFT address. If no Place for presentation is indicated in this field, the Guarantor's place of issue indicated above shall be the Place for presentation*]
- **EXPIRY:** [*Insert expiry date or describe expiry event*]
- **THE PARTY LIABLE FOR THE PAYMENT OF ANY CHARGES:** [*Insert the name of the party*]

As Guarantor, we hereby irrevocably undertake to pay the Beneficiary any amount up to the Guarantee Amount upon presentation of the Beneficiary's complying demand, in the form of presentation indicated above, supported by such other documents as may be listed above and in any event by the Beneficiary's statement, whether in the demand itself or in a separate signed document accompanying or identifying the demand, indicating in what respect the Applicant is in breach of its obligations under the Underlying Relationship.

Any demand under this Guarantee must be received by us on or before Expiry at the Place for presentation indicated above.

THIS GUARANTEE IS SUBJECT TO THE UNIFORM RULES FOR DEMAND GUARANTEES (URDG) 2010 REVISION, ICC PUBLICATION No. 758.

SIGNATURE(S)

## Optional clauses to be Inserted in the Form of Demand Guarantee

- **Time as from which a demand can be presented if different from the date of issue:**

A demand under this guarantee may be presented as from [*indicate date or event,* e.g.:

- The crediting of [*insert currency and exact amount to be received as advance payment*] to the applicant's account [*i n d i c a t e   a c c o u n t   n u m b e r*] m a i n t a i n e d with the guarantor, provided such remittance identifies the guarantee to which it relates;

- The receipt by the guarantor of [*insert currency and exact amount to be received as advance payment*] for further credit to the applicant's account [*indicate account number*] maintained with the guarantor, provided such remittance identifies the guarantee to which it relates;*or

- The presentation to the guarantor of a statement stating [*the release of the tender guarantee*] [*the issue of a documentary credit fulfilling the following terms: indicate amount, issuing or confirming party and goods/services description*] or [*the entry into effect of the underlying contract*].

- **Variation of amount clause:**

❖ The Guarantee Amount will be **reduced** by [*insert percentage of Guarantee Amount or exact amount and currency*] upon [*choose one or more of the options below*:

- Presentation to the Guarantor of the following document(s): [*insert list of documents*];

- In the case of an index specified in the guarantee as triggering reduction [*insert index figure triggering the reduction in the Guarantee Amount*]; or

- (In the case of a payment guarantee): the remittance of [*insert exact amount and currency*] to the beneficiary's account [*indicate account number*] held with the guarantor, provided the record of such remittance enables the guarantor to identify the guarantee to which it relates (for example, by referring to the guarantee's reference number).]

---

* This suggested operativeness/entry into effect clause, like the one in the bullet immediately preceding it, is frequently used in advance payment and retention money guarantees. In both cases, the clause ensures that the guarantee is not available for drawdown before the amount due by the beneficiary under the underlying contract is paid to the applicant. There are two ways to draft this clause. The first one, reflected in the first bullet, is to consider the guarantee operative only when the amount is effectively credited to the applicant's account. This leaves the beneficiary/payor with the risks of errors in credit transfers or third party attachments. Another way to draft this type of clauses, reflected in the second bullet, considers the beneficiary's obligations as satisfied when the payment is received by the guarantor holding the applicant's account. Any delay in crediting that payment to the applicant's account is left to be sorted out between the applicant and the guarantor according to the bank-customer relationship agreement or rules of law.

❖ The Guarantee Amount will be **increased** by [*insert percentage or exact amount and currency*] upon [*choose one or more of the options below*:

- Presentation to the Guarantor of the following document(s): [*insert list of documents*];

- Presentation to the Guarantor of the Applicant's statement stating that the underlying contract was amended to increase the scope or value of the works and specifying the amount and currency of the new value; or

- In the case of an index specified in the guarantee as triggering increase [*insert index figure triggering increase in the Guarantee Amount*].]

- **Sample terms for article 15(a)'s supporting statement to be provided by the beneficiary:**

❖ In the case of a **tender guarantee**, the supporting statement could state:

The Applicant:

- Has withdrawn its offer during the tender period, or

- While it was declared the successful bidder, the Applicant did not sign the contract corresponding to its offer and/or failed to provide the guarantee(s) requested in the call for tenders.

❖ In the case of a **performance guarantee**, the supporting statement could state:

The Applicant is in breach of its obligations with respect to the underlying relationship because [*of late delivery*] [*the contract's performance was not completed by the due date*] [*there was a shortfall in the quantity of the goods supplied under the contract*] [*the delivered works are defective*] etc.

❖ In the case of a **payment guarantee**, the supporting statement could state:

The Applicant has not fulfilled its contractual payment obligations.

❖ Supporting statements required under **other types of guarantees** (advance payment, retention money, delivery, warranty, maintenance, etc.) are likewise expected to be general in their drafting without the need for the beneficiary to substantiate its claim or to provide meticulous technical detail of the breach absent an express requirement in the guarantee itself.

## Form of Counter-Guarantee under URDG 758

*[Counter-guarantor Letterhead or SWIFT identifier Code]*

To: *[Insert name and contact information of Guarantor]*

Date: *[Insert date of issue]*

**Please issue under our responsibility in favour of the Beneficiary your guarantee in the following wording:**

*[Quote the following Form of Demand Guarantee under URDG 758, provide brief details of the guarantee or use your own guarantee text as appropriate]*

- **Type of guarantee:** *[Specify tender guarantee, advance payment guarantee, performance guarantee, payment guarantee, retention money guarantee, warranty guarantee, etc.]*
- **Guarantee No.** *[Guarantor to insert guarantee reference number]*
- **The Guarantor:** *[Guarantor to insert name and address of place of issue, unless indicated in the addressee field above]*
- **The Applicant:** *[Insert name and address]*
- **The Beneficiary:** *[Insert name and address]*
- **The Underlying Relationship:** The Applicant's obligation in respect of *[Insert reference number or other information identifying the contract, tender conditions or other relationship between the applicant and the beneficiary on which the guarantee is based]*
- **Guarantee Amount and currency:** *[Insert in figures and words the maximum amount payable and the currency in which it is payable]*
- **Any document required in support of the demand for payment, apart from the supporting statement that is explicitly required in the text below:** *[Insert any additional document required in support of the demand for payment. If the guarantee requires no documents other than the demand and the supporting statement, keep this space empty or indicate "none"]*
- **Language of any required documents:** *[Insert the language of any required document. Documents to be issued by the applicant or the beneficiary shall be in the language of the guarantee unless otherwise indicated herein]*

- **FORM OF PRESENTATION:** [*Insert paper or electronic form. If paper, indicate mode of delivery. If electronic, indicate the format, the system for data delivery and the electronic address for presentation*]
- **PLACE FOR PRESENTATION:** [*Guarantor to insert address of branch where a paper presentation is to be made or, in the case of an electronic presentation, an electronic address such as the Guarantor's SWIFT address. If no Place for presentation is indicated in this field, the Guarantor's place of issue indicated above shall be the Place for presentation*]
- **EXPIRY OF GUARANTEE:** [*Insert expiry date or describe expiry event*]
- **THE PARTY LIABLE FOR THE PAYMENT OF ANY CHARGES:** [*Insert the name of the party*]

As Guarantor, we hereby irrevocably undertake to pay the Beneficiary any amount up to the Guarantee Amount upon presentation of the Beneficiary's complying demand, in the form of presentation indicated above, supported by such other documents as may be listed above and in any event by the Beneficiary's statement, whether in the demand itself or in a separate signed document accompanying or identifying the demand, indicating in what respect the Applicant is in breach of its obligations under the Underlying Relationship.

Any demand under this Guarantee must be received by us on or before Expiry at the Place for presentation indicated above.

**THIS GUARANTEE IS SUBJECT TO THE UNIFORM RULES FOR DEMAND GUARANTEES (URDG) 2010 REVISION, ICC PUBLICATION NO. 758.**

[unquote]

As Counter-guarantor, we hereby irrevocably undertake to pay the Guarantor any amount up to the Counter-guarantee Amount indicated below upon presentation of the Guarantor's complying demand, in the form of presentation indicated below, supported by the Guarantor's statement, whether in the demand itself or in a separate signed document accompanying or identifying the demand, indicating that the Guarantor has received a complying demand under the guarantee.

Any demand under this Counter-guarantee must be received by us on or before Expiry of this Counter-guarantee at the place for presentation indicated below.

- **Counter-guarantee No:** [*Insert counter-guarantee reference number*]
- **The Counter-guarantor:** [*Insert name and address of place of issue, unless indicated in the letterhead*]
- **The Guarantor:** [*Insert name and address of Guarantor and place of issue of guarantee*]
- **Counter-guarantee Amount and currency:** [*Insert in figures and words the maximum amount payable and the currency in which it is payable*]
- **Form of presentation:** [*Insert paper or electronic form. If paper, indicate mode of delivery. If electronic, indicate the format, the system for data delivery and the electronic address for presentation*]
- **Place for presentation:** [*Counter-guarantor to insert address of branch where a paper presentation is to be made or, in the case of an electronic presentation, an electronic address such as the counter-guarantor's SWIFT address. If no Place for presentation is indicated in this field, the Counter-guarantor's place of issue indicated above shall be the Place for presentation*]
- **Expiry of counter-guarantee:** [*Insert expiry date or describe expiry event. Note that the expiry of the counter-guarantee is generally scheduled to occur later than the expiry of the guarantee to include a mailing period*]
- **The party liable for the payment of any charges:** [*Insert the name of the party, generally the counter-guarantor*]

The Guarantor is requested to confirm to the Counter-guarantor the issuance of the guarantee.

**This Counter-guarantee is subject to the Uniform Rules for Demand Guarantees (URDG) 2010 revision, ICC Publication No. 758.**

Signature(s)

# ICC TASK FORCE ON GUARANTEES

## Terms of Reference

1. The Task Force on Guarantees is an ICC forum for experts that aims to pool ideas and impact new policy on practical issues relating to international guarantees. It is created for an initial term of three years that is automatically renewable for successive equal terms unless the Task Force on Guarantees or ICC Banking Commission votes for its dissolution.

2. Membership of the Task Force on Guarantees is open to members of ICC, including members of the Banking Commission, the Commission on Commercial Law and Practice and the Commission on Financial Services and Insurance. Non-ICC members who represent professional organizations with relevant expertise can request to participate as observers to the work of the Task Force on Guarantees.

3. The principal assignment of the Task Force on Guarantees is to promote a wider use of the Uniform Rules for Demand Guarantees (URDG) in all business sectors and geographical regions. This will be accomplished, among other means, through the regular organization of, or participation in, dedicated local, regional and international seminars and roundtables with professional federations and international organizations, as well as by authoring dedicated publications. More generally, the Task Force on Guarantees will monitor international guarantee practice, relating court and arbitral decisions, national laws and regulations as well as the work of other international and regional organizations in the area of guarantees.

4. The Task Force will also consider and propose to relevant ICC commissions and councils other work that should be undertaken by ICC in the field of guarantees.

5. The Task Force on Guarantees will assist the technical adviser of the ICC Banking Commission in answering any query relating to URDG, as well as in performing the role ascribed to the technical adviser in the DOCDEX rules.

6. If so requested by an ICC commission, council or the secretariat of the International Court of Arbitration, the Task Force on Guarantees will address any query regarding guarantees, including other ICC rules on guarantees such as the Uniform Rules for Contract Bonds, in order to ensure consistency in the position of ICC vis-à-vis practices relating to the different types of guarantees and coordinate a joint promotion of all ICC rules and support services in the matter of guarantees.

7. The Task Force on Guarantees will regularly report to the ICC Banking Commission about its activity and, where relevant or if so requested, to other ICC commissions or councils as well.

8. The Task Force on Guarantees will meet at least once a year and whenever invited by the Chairman of the Task Force on Guarantees. No minimum number of participants is required to hold a valid meeting of the Task Force.

9. The secretariat of the ICC Banking Commission will also act as the secretariat for the Task Force.

**Membership:**

Georges Affaki (**Chair,** France), Karin Bachmayer (Austria), Roeland Bertrams (Netherlands), Rolf J. Breisig (Germany), Maximilian Burger-Scheidlin (Austria), Mohammad M. Burjaq (Jordan), Carlo Calosso (Italy), Roger F. Carouge (Germany), Gabriel Chami (Lebanon), Haluk Erdemol (Turkey), Thomas B. Felsberg (Brazil), Xavier Fornt (Spain), Michel Gally (France), Sir Roy Goode (United Kingdom), Andrea Hauptmann (Austria), Khaled Kawan (Bahrain), György Lampert (Hungary), Fredrik Lundberg (Sweden), Robert Marchal (Belgium), Mi Na (China), Antonio Maximiano Nicoletti (Brazil), Eva Oszi-Migléczi (Hungary), Sae Woon Park (Republic of Korea), Christoph Martin Radtke (France), Natalia A. Rannikh (Russian Federation), Glenn Ransier (United States), Kate Richardson (United Kingdom), Zuzana Rollova (Czech Republic), Cristina Rooth (Sweden), Don Smith (United States), Jeremy Smith (United Kingdom), Shri K.N. Suvarna (India), Pradeep Taneja (Bahrain), Farideh Tazhibi (Islamic Republic of Iran), Pieris Theodorou (Cyprus), Edward Verhey (Netherlands), Antonella Zanaboni (Italy).

**Observers:**

Wilko Gunster (ICC Netherlands), Alison Micheli (the World Bank), Jean-Jacques Verdeaux (the World Bank).

## DOCDEX: A service tailored to resolving URDG disputes

The ICC Documentary Instruments Dispute Resolution Expertise (DOCDEX) Rules provide an alternative dispute resolution procedure for settling disputes. They lead to an **independent, impartial and prompt** expert decision.

**Applicability:** DOCDEX dispute resolution is applicable to disputes relating to any of the following sets of rules:

- ❖ ICC Uniform Rules for Demand Guarantees (URDG)
- ❖ ICC Uniform Customs and Practice for Documentary Credits(UCP)
- ❖ ICC Uniform Rules for Bank-to-Bank Reimbursements under Documentary Credits (URR)
- ❖ ICC Uniform Rules for Collections (URC)

**Procedure:** The party initiating a DOCDEX procedure must file its Request with the ICC International Centre for Expertise ("Centre"). The Centre will invite the responding party/parties to file an Answer within a maximum of 30 days. The Centre will then promptly appoint three experts ("Appointed Experts").

The Appointed Experts render their decision ("DOCDEX Decision") within 30 days of receiving all the documentation relating to the case. There are no hearings.

**Quality control:** Upon receipt of the DOCDEX Decision, the Centre has it reviewed by the Technical Adviser of the ICC Banking Commission or his nominated delegate to ascertain whether it is in line with the applicable ICC Rules and their interpretation by the ICC Banking Commission. Any amendments suggested by the Technical Adviser or his delegate are subject to acceptance by a majority of the Appointed Experts.

**Experts:** The Appointed Experts are chosen by the Centre from a list maintained by the ICC Banking Commission. The list includes international experts from all over the world with extensive experience and knowledge of the applicable ICC Rules. The names of the Appointed Experts are not disclosed to the parties.

**Nature of the decision:** The DOCDEX Decision is not binding on the parties, unless they agree otherwise. However, it gives them a strong evaluation of their case and can encourage an amicable and final settlement of the dispute.

**Timing:** The parties usually receive the DOCDEX Decision within 60 days of the filing of the initial Request.

**Costs:** The Standard Fee is US$ 5,000. In exceptional cases an Additional Fee of up to US$ 5,000 can be requested. The total cost of a DOCDEX Decision will never exceed US$ 10,000.

The DOCDEX Rules are available at **www.iccdocdex.org**

DOCDEX is made available by the International Chamber of Commerce (ICC) through its International Centre for Expertise (Centre) in association with the ICC Commission on Banking Technique and Practice.

**Contact:**

ICC International Centre for Expertise

38, Cours Albert 1er

75008 Paris

France

Tel : +33 1 49 53 30 53

Fax : +33 1 49 53 30 49

Email : docdex@iccwbo.org

# ICC at a Glance

ICC is the world business organization, a representative body that speaks with authority on behalf of enterprises from all sectors in every part of the world.

The fundamental mission of ICC is to promote trade and investment across frontiers and help business corporations meet the challenges and opportunities of globalization. Its conviction that trade is a powerful force for peace and prosperity dates from the organization's origins early in the last century. The small group of far-sighted business leaders who founded ICC called themselves "the merchants of peace".

Because its member companies and associations are themselves engaged in international business, ICC has unrivalled authority in making rules that govern the conduct of business across borders. Although these rules are voluntary, they are observed in countless thousands of transactions every day and have become part of the fabric of international trade.

ICC also provides essential services, foremost among them the ICC International Court of Arbitration, the world's leading arbitral institution. Another service is the World Chambers Federation, ICC's worldwide network of chambers of commerce, fostering interaction and exchange of chamber best practice.

Within a year of the creation of the United Nations, ICC was granted consultative status at the highest level with the UN and its specialized agencies.

Business leaders and experts drawn from the ICC membership establish the business stance on broad issues of trade and investment policy as well as on vital technical and sectoral subjects. These include financial services, information technologies, telecommunications, marketing ethics, the environment, transportation, competition law and intellectual property.

ICC was founded in 1919. Today it groups thousands of member companies and associations from over 130 countries. National committees work with their members to address the concerns of business in their countries and convey to their governments the business views formulated by ICC.

# Some ICC Specialized Divisions

- ❖ ICC International Court of Arbitration (Paris)
- ❖ ICC International Centre for Expertise (Paris)
- ❖ ICC World Chambers Federation (Paris)
- ❖ ICC Institute of World Business Law (Paris)
- ❖ ICC Centre for Maritime Co-operation (London)
- ❖ ICC Commercial Crime Services (London)
- ❖ ICC Services (Paris)

❖ **Publications**

ICC Publications Department is committed to offering the best resources on business and trade for the international community.

The content of ICC publications is derived from the work of ICC commissions, institutions and individual international experts. The specialized list covers a range of topics including international banking, international trade reference and terms (Incoterms), law and arbitration, counterfeiting and fraud, model commercial contracts and environmental issues.

Publications are available in both traditional paper and electronic formats from the ICC Business Bookstore.

❖ **Events**

ICC's programme of conferences and seminars is the essential channel for passing on the world business organization's expertise to a wider audience.

ICC Events, a Department of ICC Services, spotlights policy issues of direct concern to business such as banking techniques and practices, e-business, IT and telecoms, piracy and counterfeiting.

ICC Events also runs training courses on international arbitration and negotiating international contracts for business people, corporate counsel, lawyers and legal practitioners involved in international trade.

## Source Products for Global Business

ICC's specialized list of publications covers a range of topics including international banking, international trade reference and terms (Incoterms), law and arbitration, counterfeiting and fraud, model commercial contracts and environmental issues.

ICC products are available from ICC national committees which exist in over 80 countries around the world. Contact details for a national committee in your country are available at **www.iccwbo.org**

You may also order ICC products online from the ICC Business Bookstore at **www.iccbooks.com**

## ICC Publications

38 Cours Albert 1er
75008 Paris
France
Tel.     +33 1 49 53 29 23
Fax      +33 1 49 53 29 02
e-mail   pub@iccwbo.org